DEPLOYED WITH MY MOTHER

a memoir

DAVID WEILL

WITH TAMMY CHANDLER

WordCrafts

Published by WordCrafts Press
Cody, Wyoming 82414
www.wordcrafts.net

To my mother
who taught me how
to make everything possible

Contents

Not my plan. Ever have anything not going according to plan? Welcome to my life.

I wrote this book to give my perspective on what it was like to go to war with my mother and to share personal struggles, add a little humor, and pass along some hope and encouragement. The stories in this book are snapshots of what happened during the time I was in the desert with my mom, and how God used each detour to lead me to a relationship of hope and peace with Him. As you read, I want *you* to have hope and be able to find a unique perspective when things don't go according to plan.

My prayer is that as you read this book, you will find things that relate to your life. Maybe you've never been to war—maybe you have—but as you read, may you find things that encourage you, make you laugh, maybe make you cry, but most of all, may you find the hope that Jesus offers to all of us. No matter what our desert may look like, no matter what comes, or when things don't go according to plan—we have hope. Welcome to my desert journey.

Blessings,

Dave

G rowing up is something that all of us have to do, but each life has its own unique experiences. I had the privilege of growing up with a loving, go-getter type mom and a younger sister.

My parents got divorced when I was about five years old, and my Dad moved to the Washington, D.C. area. Phone calls were hardly ever made, and contact was at a minimum. My parents had argued a lot before my dad left, but I still hoped he would want to be a part of my life. As contact and visits grew less and less, my expectations dwindled from hoping to see him, to hoping for a phone call. Time passed, and the phone calls didn't come. This became my new reality. As each new birthday rolled around, I hoped for a small gift—but they never came. Maybe he couldn't afford one. I would hope for a card for my birthday. Nothing came in the mail. As each birthday came and went, it got to the point that I lowered my expectation to thinking at least he would call on my special day. But the phone never rang. With each disappointment, my resentment toward my dad grew, and I became increasingly wounded. In a weird way, I thought this was normal because I didn't know anything different, and it fostered a bitterness in my heart I didn't even realize was there until much later in my life.

My mom worked as a maid cleaning houses. There wasn't much money in it, but it was enough to get us by. And by getting by, I mean there was food on our table—at least most times—and a roof over our heads. As a young child, my mom would have to take me to work with her because there wasn't really money for a babysitter. I did my best to stay out of the way and be helpful when I could, but I also remember seeing all the things that other people had. One time, I was so enthralled with the pool at one home that I threw wood chips in it to see if they would float! I don't remember if my mom ever took me back to that house, or if Mom ever got to go back and work there, but I never did throw chips in a pool again. I started to realize that there were people who had everything—at least what a small boy's mind thought was everything. I knew there was no extra for us, because we barely had enough. As a child, a mindset that I didn't ever want to go without was formed and cemented in my young brain.

I distinctly remember people bringing us food for Thanksgiving, and as I got older, I was able to look back and see that we were probably the family that others in the neighborhood considered to be poor. We wore the hand-me-downs from others, and we had to accept charity in order to have things. I remember one time we were traveling in our run-down car, and it died. We were stranded in an unfamiliar town with no money, and I could tell my mom was distressed. She found the mechanic in town, and we walked to his garage. My mom bargained with the mechanic and sold him her Amway products that were in the trunk of the car to get it fixed.

My mom would not take no for an answer, and she was creative in finding solutions to her problems. I took my mom's example of determination and would remember her creativity when I faced obstacles. She later replaced the products that she had borrowed from Amway to get the car repaired, and I remember the toll it took on her to get that done. I am grateful, looking back, that a mechanic was willing to take products he probably didn't need to help a family that had no way to pay. Events like these began the process in my own heart of wanting to help others. Instead of being the beneficiary of others' kindness, I wanted to become the benefactor. I wanted to be generous, and in my thinking, that required having money.

Because of our situation, we did life differently. I remember for one birthday in particular, I wanted to give each of my classmates an individual bag of M&Ms. Each time we went to the grocery store, we were able to purchase one more bag. At last the time came to take those packets of chocolatey goodness to school to share I had just enough to give one to every classmate and still have one packet left for me. It was the perfect plan! And it worked perfectly until one last kid said he didn't get one. So I gave it to him. It was just one more example of having almost enough.

My mom went without some things, just so I could have a party at recess. Even though I didn't get to eat a bag of those M&Ms because there were only enough for my classmates, I never told my mom. I didn't want her to feel badly about it. I was just thrilled I got to celebrate my birthday with my classmates on the playground that year.

I learned to root for the underdog, to cheer for the longshot—even if that person was me. I still root for the underdog, whether it's in a sports game or in life. That memory has stuck with me through all of these years, and M&Ms are still one of my comfort foods. I jokingly refer to them as "diet pills" because I eat them when I get stressed, and I can stick to a single packet, instead of eating a whole bag.

I tried to be a generous child, but there wasn't money in the budget for me to purchase gifts, so I would *borrow* them—or barter for them. I never liked the feeling of being broke. One Christmas, I snuck into my sister's room when she wasn't home, so that I could get a book. I wrapped it up and gave it to her for Christmas, just so there was something from me for her under the tree. The mindset I learned was generosity was vital to being a good person and feeling good about myself. I rationalized that my desire for money was a goal in life—I wanted money so I could make other people happy. In reality, though, I wanted money to make *me* happy.

When I started fifth grade, Mom made the decision to move us from Sandy Hook, Connecticut to Tennessee. Starting over is never easy, and this move was especially hard on me. I gave up all that was familiar and comfortable. It was hard to start over with new friends, a new school, and such. I began to realize I would have to think for myself, do for myself, and be for myself, because no one else was going to be there for me—except my mom and my annoying sister.

I kept to myself, even at the age of ten, and I started building walls. Walls were safer than bridges, because walls kept the hurt out. I didn't like the feeling of loneliness, but it was better than low-down hurt. I began the mindset of keeping people at a distance. I was funny, so I didn't have to withdraw, just always stayed guarded. I longed to belong, but I had already decided it was better to keep that feeling locked up. I had to be strong for myself and for my mom and sister regardless of how I felt on the inside. I didn't realize at the time that those feelings would make my journey to hope harder, longer, and very difficult.

My mom decided the Boy Scouts would be a good experience for me in middle school. I was excited to become a part of something—to belong—so I behaved myself, learned discipline and respect, and worked hard to become a good scout. One of the highlights from my time in the scouts was going to the 1985 Jamboree and seeing the Beach Boys and Nancy Reagan. One winter, our scout troop was supposed to lead a church service on a Sunday morning, and I was excited. The night before, however, there was a blizzard. Wind howling, snow streaming down, the ground was covered in a menace of white and ice. The roads were barely passable, but my mother was determined I was going to make it to that church service to speak and to pray. We bundled up in the few warm clothes and jackets that we had, and we walked over a mile to the main road, where my mom flagged down a driver and told him about the service. He agreed to take me, and my mother put me in a car with a stranger who drove me to church. Understand, those were very different times than now, and we lived in rural Tennessee, but I am still thankful that my story did not end in the roadside ditch with a crazy driver or a psychopath who abducted children in a blizzard! I made it to the church, I did pray and speak, and my Scoutmaster gave me a ride home.

My mom got me there. She did what she had to do.

Two mindsets developed in me during those years. First, never makes excuses, and second, do whatever it takes to make things happen. My mom set the example of both of these qualities in my life. She just believed that you always persevere, and you always push through, no excuses, no complaining. Her dynamic, determined spirit instilled in me the desire to become the best I could without making any excuses. Because of her support, I went on to earn the rank of Eagle Scout. I also learned to not ever make someone else feel bad when they were doing the best they could. I learned this from watching the sacrifices and the decisions my mom made, and this worked in my life to develop mercy—but that story comes later.

One of the reasons we moved to Tennessee was to be closer to my grandparents so they could help with our care when Mom had to work. My sister, April, and I were typical siblings. We fought like cats and dogs at times. The problem was we just didn't really have much in common. We were so very different, but we did learn over time to have each other's backs. We grew to learn how to protect each other, even if there were times, we didn't really like each other. We were family, and family matters. Our grandparents were wise to allow us to work out our differences and come to realize the importance of being family. They loved us, even when we were not getting along with each other.

Money

When I got into upper elementary school, I had a handheld basketball video game that made beeping noises when the buttons were pushed. It was an older model, but I was impressed with the novelty of having it, and I figured out that classmates would pay fifteen cents a game to play it, and that was the beginning of my entrepreneurial mindset. I was determined to find ways to be able to get money to feed the mindset that money would make me happy. Money itself wasn't the problem—my growing love for it was.

While my love for money increased, I was also a bit of a cheapskate. As a young teenager, I really wanted to play an arcade game but did not have the money. I am embarrassed now to admit it, but I collected twenty-five pennies from the fountain at the World's Fair, then made my way to the souvenir shop to exchange the pennies for a quarter. I did not want to be the guy who was left out because he didn't have money to spend. I had determined that what I did wasn't *really* wrong, because those people had discarded that money, and I *worked* to collect it. It is one small example of how I did whatever it took to get what I wanted. In my mind, the end justified the means, and this would lead to problems later in my life.

All these experiences led me to believe that money was the key to happiness. I figured if I could just get my hands on enough money, I would be able to solve all my problems—and all my mom's problems—and we could be happy and secure. If I just had enough money I could prove I wasn't poor. The problem with that mindset was that it all depended on what *I* could do. It was the *I, me, my* mindset, and that would prove to be a greater problem in the future than being poor as a child ever was.

In time, I would learn that money doesn't solve anything. No matter how much I had, it was never enough. I believed the myth that more money equated to more happiness, and I was going to pursue it, no matter the cost. But all money did was keep me chasing my own tail. I didn't understand that money is really about management—stewardship. If you can't manage what you have when you have little, you won't manage it well when you have much. And it won't matter how much you have, you will still want more. I didn't understand that rich people have the same problems as poor people—they just deal with more zeroes at the end of their bank accounts.

At this point in my life, I didn't care. I believed money would solve all my problems, and it didn't matter to me what it would take to get to where I thought I was going.

The world is going to throw obstacles and issues at all of us. It might be a blizzard, a car that breaks down in a strange town or a plethora of other challenges. Regardless of the circumstances, when those obstacles come, each of us have a choice to make. We can get discouraged, bitter, and withdrawn, or we can be determined, creative, and persistent. Mindsets can be opportunities, or they can be obstacles. It is important to evaluate them all and determine which ones are true and which ones are holding us back.

I didn't grow up going to church, but once we moved to east Tennessee and closer to my grandparents, I developed a *drug* problem. It wasn't marijuana or cocaine, it was that my grandparents, Arville and Mary, *drug* me to church.

Attending church certainly wasn't my idea. I wasn't particularly excited about getting dressed up in stiff clothes and going down the street to be bored to death—my thinking as a fifth grader. I felt like I was different from the other kids, because I had no idea who Moses was, or Paul, or even Jesus for that matter. After a while though, I got used to it and I learned the fine art of faking it. I went along with the crowd and played the game pretty well.

Before long, I figured I was a Christian because I went to church, was a good person for the most part, and played the game so well. I had even deceived myself. My sister and I were sometimes mischievous. She always got caught, but because I was so good at playing the roll of a *good Christian boy*, no one suspected me of any shenanigans. I thought that was quite funny, but while I looked good on the outside, it couldn't fill the empty space on the inside. It couldn't replace the bitterness and hurt that was growing inside. But I still managed to keep it hidden from others.

I am grateful that my grandparents did drag me to church; I just wish someone would have seen through the façade sooner. I wish someone would have touched my heart with relationship and shared with me that God wanted to be my Father—a truly good, loving Father—and that Jesus wanted to be my Savior, my rescue from the eternal future of separation with God. Thankfully, my grandparents stuck with me through all of my antics and game playing. They would eventually pray me through the desert and into God's kingdom. But it would take time.

High school was easy for me in the sense that I did not worry about my grades. I did what was required of me, but I didn't worry about trying to get into an ivy league school.

My mom, on the other hand, had already fought her way through working full-time, being a full-time single mother, and going to school to become a nurse. I admired her for going after something that made her life better, but it sure was hard work! I graduated from Elizabethon High School in 1988. Since there had not been any major skirmishes that I knew about, I explored the idea of joining the Army. When the recruiter called, we talked about what I could do.

He suggested that I become a cook.

I didn't want to be a cook. My cooking rationale was that if it took more than ninety seconds to make a meal, it wasn't worth it. I enjoyed eating, but I would rather spend my time doing pretty much anything other than cooking. Instead I would just grab a sandwich or a bowl of cereal and move on to the next thing. My logic at the time, even though it was terrible as I look back on it, was if I never got married, I'd better learn how to cook.

Then the recruiter told me that my time served would provide money for college. I went home and waited for Mom so we could discuss the offer.

"Hey, Mom. Do you think I should join the Army?"

"No."

Our conversation took less than thirty seconds.

Then my mindset kicked in—my *money* mindset. I thought if I could make money or save money by joining the Army, I wanted to give it a try. There was also the obvious pride in serving our country, but mostly I was serving myself. The deciding factor for my signing up was based on what the recruiter told me about it helping to pay for college. I explained to my mom the financial benefits of joining the Army.

Besides there were no major wars going on at that time. The thought of war never even crossed my mind. Think about that for a second. The desire for money had so warped my thinking that it never occurred to me that as a soldier, my primary function was to be a warrior—to be ready to go to war.

My argument must have won my mom over, because after she thought about it, she said, "Okay." And I signed up.

I started college at East Tennessee State University and completed a full semester, with good grades, before I shipped out. I minored in Business—what else would motivate me to study but the thought of making more money? I figured I would just serve my one weekend a month and two weeks in the summer, and it would all be good. The thought of going to war never crossed my mind as a possibility. I suppose I was naïve.

On December 27, 1988, I shipped out to Ft. Bliss, Texas, for Basic Training.

I did not prepare for Basic Training like I should have, because I didn't really understand what it was going to take to survive it.

One night after I had signed up, but before I went to Basic, my best friend, Kevin, and I watched the movie *Rocky*. When it was over, it was close to midnight, but we were so motivated and inspired that we decided to drive down to Elizabethon High School and run a mile on the track to prepare for Basic. Obviously, that single one mile run did little to prepare me for Basic Training.

My first two-mile run at Basic left me sucking wind, and I couldn't even finish it without stopping. Of course, that brought on the ire of the Drill Sergeant, and I realized quickly I was going to have to be motivated and disciplined to make it in that place. Kevin also ended up joining the service after that run, but he wound up in a different unit.

Upon arrival at Basic we were subjected to a battery of tests. One was the vision test. I thought it was a waste of time. I could see just fine. But there were no exceptions, everyone was required to have their eyes examined. Two weeks later, there was a box on my bunk, and it had my name on it. Normally, we were excited to get packages during Basic Training, but this one did not contain cookies or letters from home. It held glasses. Glasses! I'd never worn glasses before.

The Army only had one style of frames for its GI-issued glasses. They were called BC (Birth Control) glasses, because they were so ugly they tended to prevent any dates from happening.

Just what I need, I thought, *uniform glasses issued by the Army. Why? I can see just fine, and they definitely are not going to make me more attractive.*

But I put them on just to see what would happen, and *whoa!* I only *thought* I could see before. Now I could see vibrant colors, blades of grass, facial expressions, even details like crumbs on the floor of the mess hall. Who knew how long my vision had been impaired, and I didn't know it? How many years had I gone with blurred vision thinking this was normal? I had never realized that I needed vision correction. I got excited about the new details I could see and how clear my vision became with the help of my glasses.

My original perspective was that I was just fine, but somebody took the time to run a test and prescribe some truth into my life, and my perspective changed. I am so thankful to the Army for doing the vision test. Not only did my perspective change, but my whole life was changed just by being able to see clearly.

Sometimes God does the same thing to us in life. We think our perspective is just fine, nobody needs to interfere with our plans, and we don't need to change our attitudes. But the glasses of truth come out, and if we take the time to put them on, we find ourselves seeing details and expressions we never saw before. We change the way we look at things, and that changes our entire lives. I thought the Army was just a meal ticket to college, but it would turn out to be the second-most-important decision I ever made in my life. Accepting Christ was the most important—even though this would not happen until much later—and the Army was second, because God used my time in the Army to totally change my mindset.

When was the last time you had a new perspective? Maybe you too got new physical glasses, and you were able to see details you hadn't noticed before. And as great as the physical reaction is to this sudden clarity of vision, the truth is, we all need a spiritual eye exam. We all need to be sure that truth is the lens that we are looking through when it comes to life. Just imagine what all we might be missing out on simply because we are unwilling to look through the lens of truth?

†††

Mom sent the best oatmeal raisin cookies anyone had ever tasted. Our family has a secret recipe that has been passed down through the generations, and these are the best cookies! I have thought about partnering with a snack company to bring these cookies to the world. Mom inherited the recipe, and she didn't send just one batch. She would light up the barracks with her cookies throughout my basic training. Mom always went above and beyond to let me know that she was thinking of me and had my back. These cookies are dangerous because you cannot stop eating them—they should come with a warning. They are that good.

The rule about care packages was that whatever was in them that was edible had to be gone by morning. It was supposed to promote comradery and sharing among the unit, but not for me. I was still highly motivated by money. Forget sharing! I took my cookies to a nearby empty barrack and hid them. After I finished eating the whole cookies, I bagged up the leftover cookie crumbles. I could get ten dollars for each Ziplock bag of crumbs. I never missed an opportunity to cash in.

I was so motivated by money that I was willing to almost starve myself to make a dollar. While we were out in the field, I would actually sneak an orange from breakfast and save it for lunch so I could sell my MRE (meal ready to eat) to make some extra cash. As I recall, the rule was that soldiers could not have more than fifty dollars in their wallets at any given time. Our drill sergeant told us, "You belong to us now." There were only three things they could not do to us during Basic Training, he told us. They couldn't have sex with us, they could not physically hit us, and they could not take our money—everything else was fair game. I figured, since they couldn't take it from me, I'd get as much as I could for the MREs.

One day out in the field, the drill sergeant came up to me and said, "Weill, let's see what's in your wallet."

My heart raced, because I knew what I had been doing, and I knew he had found out. I had over $200 in my wallet. Later that night he called for me and told me to get a shovel and start digging a hole big enough for a man. I thought I might be digging my own grave, but I did as I was told. When I finished, I went and found him and told him it was done.

He said, "Bury your orange."

I went out, put the orange in the hole, and filled it all in. I reported back to him that I was finished.

"Good."

He didn't even bother to go see the hole, or that it was filled in, but the message was loud and clear: *Bury your desire to bend the rules for your love of money, David.*

I needed to learn that sometimes the hole I was digging was one that I wouldn't get out of easily. I needed to be careful to not allow worldly desires to deviate me from doing what is right.

Mom's Sign Up

After I got back from Basic Training, life fell into a new routine. I lived at home, worked, and went to the Army Reserves on my assigned weekends.

I had always wanted to be a good kid, even if sometimes I did find mischief or get into trouble. I had a desire to obey my mom, to love her, and do my best so she would be proud of me. Signing up for the Army Reserves had been my way to pay my own college expenses, and she appreciated that. If I took care of my college, she wouldn't have that burden, and that was important to me. After raising two children pretty much on her own and doing all she could, my mom had been through enough, and anything I could do to help was going to get done.

My sister and I probably grew up quicker than most kids, and I learned to take initiative and make things happen. God has a way of making sure we have what we need when we need it. In my case, He gave me a glimpse of what was just around the corner by allowing me to see how Mom handled my joining the Reserves.

Fast forward a few months. I learned that they let *old* people in the Army if they have advanced medical training.

Since my mom was a nurse and at the ripe old age of forty, I said, "Hey, Mom, they let old people in the Army. They have a special boot camp for you. Want to join?"

The conversation lasted a little less than thirty seconds, and you probably already know what she said. Since then, my perspective has changed greatly. Now that I'm in my fifties, I am thinking that she was the perfect age, and I was too young. So many things change based on your perspective. Many times, a change of perspective can take something negative and make it positive just by looking at it from a different point of view. Had I seen my mom as the capable medical professional she was, perhaps I wouldn't have seen her as *old*. Now I can see that she had experiences and training that made her more mature and prepared for being deployed than I was.

Because Mom had done the hard work of nursing school, she could enlist as an officer, and her Basic Training would be a lot less intense than mine had been. There were perks too. Steady paycheck, respect, and we could work together in the same unit. Since there was no thought of being deployed in either of our minds, she decided it would be a good idea, so she joined.

I was glad to do the Army together. We both thought serving our country would be a good idea, and we both looked forward to serving together. There wasn't any big fanfare, parades, or confetti, but Mom and I celebrated after her swearing in with a small dinner, and then off she went to Basic Training.

While Mom was away, April and I took care of things at home. Our Dad's abandonment had made things hard at home on both of us. We had an unspoken understanding that we didn't talk about Dad, but we had each other's backs when push came to shove—no pun intended. We still fought on occasion. But even though she drove me crazy, as her big brother, I was determined to protect her and have her back because Dad was missing in action.

Mom finally completed Basic Training and returned home. We were once again a family unit that would be there for each other through the coming days, the coming changes, and the coming storms.

When Mom came back from Basic Training, things went back to the normal routine, except that she now went on weekend drills too. It was kind of weird at first being in the same unit as my mother, but it didn't take long to get acclimated to the situation. After all, we were both just doing our jobs.

My mom really enjoyed having our traditional roles reversed; I was cooking and providing her meals. It made me appreciate all those years that she did the cooking and provided meals, even when times were rough. It helps me even to this day to not take things for granted and be grateful.

Several times I was asked what it was like to be in the same unit as my mom, but since Mom had been such a huge part of my life growing up, this was an added bonus in my book. While some people thought we were crazy, we actually enjoyed it.

Heather, my girlfriend during this time, and her family became like a second family to me. We dated through the summer, and I really enjoyed spending time with her. She brought a softness to my life that I had not experienced before—and she liked my jokes. She was a strong person, in a good way. Heather's family lived right down the street, and our families became good friends. Her dad became a great role model for me, and I discovered through my relationship with Heather and her family that there could be a sweetness to life. We continued to enjoy our relationship as fall approached, and we looked forward to spending the holidays together.

Just before Thanksgiving, 1990, we got the call. The 912th MASH unit of Johnson City, Tennessee had been activated. Thanksgiving was a time of preparation and separation. It was a sobering holiday for all of us—Mom, April, Heather, my grandparents, and even Heather's family too. I was reeling—the timing could not have been worse. April was a senior in high school, and now not only would I be gone, but I had signed our mom up too. Now April would also be without her mother, and it was my fault.

Reality set in as I told myself that I had recruited my mom, my rock, for war, and there was nothing I could do now to change that. I went through the motions of the holiday, did my best to say the right things, be grateful on the outside for the blessings we had—things we had worked for, our family being together— but on the inside I was trying to figure it all out and control the details. I had grown adept at keeping the walls up, being guarded, protecting my turf, and I thought that was all going to have to be in overdrive now.

We were given the holiday season to be with our family. My grandparents became an integral part of our lives again as they would be the ones April would stay with while we were gone.

Heather and I were going to make it through all of this, and there would be good things to look forward to after I got back, and she would write and call. Her parents were encouraging, and her dad was someone I could look up to. We would get through this together—at least that is what we told ourselves as we sat in the living room.

We made the most of every moment, and Heather made sure to draw out my comedic side—it was important to her that I kept my sense of humor. In spite of all the separation I was feeling, Mom and I were going together. We had a bond that no one else really understood. A bond that would be tested to its core as we prepared to go to war.

November 24, 1990. We said our goodbyes, we loaded up our cars with our gear, and we were headed to Johnson City to meet the rest of our 912th MASH Unit for Deployment Preparation. The day we were to leave our unit in Johnson City to head to Ft. Bragg, we all gathered at the base, and Mom realized she left all her gear at the house! Family made a mad dash back to grab it all and got back to base before anyone up the chain could find out what she had done. It would be symbolic of things to come.

For Mom, leaving her daughter and her parents behind was difficult. Leaving them, as well as my sweetheart, made it hard on me too. The gear represented the last-ditch efforts to stay connected with them. It would be hard in the days ahead; we just didn't realize how hard.

Life is like that. We make last-ditch efforts to control situations that are beyond us. We don't understand why we have to say good-bye to loved ones, why life has to break us—crush us—at times, and we leave that one bag behind, so we can go back. One more moment, one more conversation, one more flicker of hope that life may not be as bad as it looks. We make a mad-dash to try to hold it all together, but we still find ourselves about to board the bus to leave, and there is nothing we can do about it.

But there is Someone who does have it all under control, a solid Rock, a Friend. I just wasn't ready to put my trust in Someone I couldn't see, Someone who allowed all of this to happen in my life. It would be quite some time before I was able to see that He had orchestrated every moment of my life to bring me into His unit—His forever family unit. For now, I just knew it was me and Mom going to war together.

Field Jacket

While at Fort Bragg, we were told that once we hit the desert overseas there was no more practice. Scud alarms would be the real deal. It was live ammunition, and there was no replay button like the video games I had played so many times as a kid.

We practiced relentlessly sealing our gas masks and mentally preparing for war. We were told to be prepared for anything. Mom learned these lessons the hard way. We were ordered to move out for training at a new destination, and we needed to bring our field jackets. It was warm where we were, so Mom in her *wisdom* packed light. She left her field jacket back at the barracks, because she didn't think she would need it—even though we were told to bring it. Later that day, we were transported to a thirty-degree climate change.

Guess who froze?

Because I could not let her go without a jacket, I gave her mine. I spent the training time freezing. I kept thinking over and over again, *What was I thinking asking Mom to sign up for this?*

People think it is neat that my mom and I served together, and it is, but it was also scary at times. All my growing up years, she had protected and provided for me, and now I felt it was my turn to protect her. I learned the hard way that life was not going to give me any kind of shelter, and I was going to have to find a way to make sure Mom was prepared, or we might not make it out of this thing together.

Mom learned an important lesson that day too—when you don't follow orders, other people suffer. This time it was me, but it was important to realize that following orders, obeying the instructions we were given, was imperative to surviving the war we were going into.

I would apply this truth much later, but in a spiritual way. In life, following the Bible—our field guide to real life—is also imperative to our survival. We are in a battle—a battle for our souls, minds, and hearts—and the Bible has the guidelines.

Birthday in the Army

Pearl Harbor Day happens to also be my birthday—December 7. In 1990, I turned twenty-one. and I was stationed at Ft. Bragg at the time.

My mother and a few others left for Pennsylvania for some specialized training a couple of days prior, and I was going to be without family on my birthday. My mother knew how important it was for me to be with family on my birthday. It was especially hard for her to be absent on this day because she knew how things had been with my dad being absent when I was growing up. She was sad to be away on my twenty-first.

But, you have to know my mom—she was not going to let my birthday go by unnoticed. If she couldn't be there in the flesh, what was the next best thing and only something a mother could pull off? She conspired with the First Sergeant before she left and made him promise to do something *special* for my birthday. In my mind's eye, I can still picture her negotiating with him.

On the morning of my twenty-first birthday, we were called to morning formation. I had hoped to keep this day under the radar and just celebrate by myself, but that was not to be. Our First Sergeant had promised my mom that the entire unit would sing "Happy Birthday!" at formation, and he kept the promise. He broke out leading it, and the entire unit joined in. My face was beat red, and everyone knew I was embarrassed—in a good way. I thought, *That's my mom!* Her unique personality came through even when she couldn't be there.

My earliest memories of my father were of him and my mother arguing. They divorced when I was about five.

From ages five to twenty-one, I did not see my dad much. Through all my growing up years, he only came to see us a handful of times. He got remarried and had another family, so there wasn't much time for us. As a result of his upbringing, he did not like to spend money, and he had built up a lot of trust issues.

As teenagers, my sister and I finally figured out he just didn't want to spend the money on us, or on anything for that matter. I remember wishing as a kid that my dad would simply call for my birthday. I just wanted to know that I mattered to him, but the calls never came. Neither did cards or presents.

Bitterness built up gradually, layer upon layer, as each birthday or holiday was missed without even a note or call. My heart became like a frog in a kettle. At first, the water didn't boil, it just got a little warm as the bitterness of missing out on things with my dad began to settle into my heart. It wasn't the *stuff* I wanted from him—the cards, the gifts—it was knowing that I *mattered* to him, that he connected with me. I even hoped for just a single "I love you, Son."

Even though my dad was not the kind of man I would have desired for a father, he was still my dad, and him not being present left a big hole in my life. As I got older, the kettle of bitterness got hotter and my heart grew harder.

I had heard the story of the Prodigal Son when I was a kid in

Sunday School. You know the story—the son blows all his money and makes himself an embarrassment to his family, but he goes back home, and his father welcomes him with open arms. For several years, I thought of my dad as the Prodigal Father. I kept hoping he would do right, and though I knew he and my mom would never get back together, I wanted him to ask to be a part of my life. The longer it didn't happen, the greater the canyon of bitterness and anger became in my young life. And yet, I still had a small hope that someday we would be able to get past all of that. I was willing to overlook the neglect if he was just willing to try.

Imagine my surprise when while I was busy doing my regular military duties to prepare for deployment from Ft. Bragg, and my mom came over and said, "Guess who else is here at Ft. Bragg?"

My first thought was Kevin, my best friend. But before I could answer, my mom said, "Your dad."

You could have pushed me over with a pinkie finger. I had always wanted a relationship with him, and now he was here.

Here.

At Ft. Bragg.

With us.

The reason my dad was there was because he was also in the Army—and his unit was also being deployed.

The next four days were a mix of a dream and a family reunion—sort of. We got to spend time together as a family and it was incredible. We tried to cram twenty-one years of lost time into those four days. Our hearts were happy and basking in this unlikely situation.

On Friday, January 11, 1991, we found out we had a mission number, and we would be leaving on Sunday. We alerted family about our mission, and my grandparents along with my sister decided to make a trip to see us one more time before we had to say our goodbyes and head overseas.

That Friday morning, I went to breakfast with my dad, and that night April and I stayed at a motel with our father. The unthinkable happened. I do not know how else to explain it. It was a God-thing. Call it brotherly intuition, but I could sense that something was off with my sister. Something was just not right. As I was doing the last-minute duties before deployment, I could not shake it. Even though we were leaving for war the very next day, I knew I had to talk to her.

I asked her, "Did Dad do something to you?" She stared at the ground, pain covering her face. And in an instant, I knew. She didn't say anything, and yet somehow, I knew without a single word being said. My dad had done something to my sister.

"April, look at me. What is going on?"

She looked up at me with tears and such pain in her eyes! I could tell by the look in her eyes and her physical reaction to my question that something terrible had happened. April finally admitted that my father had molested her in the hotel just the night before.

My blood began to boil! I ran my hands through my crew cut hair. I wanted to punch my fist through a wall. I grabbed my M-16, but by the grace of God, I hadn't been issued any ammunition yet. I could have easily gone to jail that day if it were not for the morals that Mom had instilled us, and the determination to make good decisions and no excuses.

I also realized I couldn't make the situation worse for April. She needed me to be her brother, not a prisoner. I was still filled with rage as we went to find Mom, then I called the MPs. It was a whirlwind from that moment on.

Chaos ensued.

That night was a blur. I needed to be with my sister, but I also had to prepare to board a plane for the desert in less than twenty-four hours.

I didn't see my dad that night, and the next day I boarded the plane and headed off to Operation Desert Storm. My mind and heart were in such inner turmoil I could hardly stand it. Two wars were happening in my life before I even set foot on the desert. Inside, my mind was full of rage and disgust, and my heart was full of guilt. After all, it would have been easy to think this was all my fault. I could have given into the lies that all of this was my fault and that had I made different choices, none of this would have happened. But that is not how life works.

I had decided to sign up for the Reserves to help pay for college. That led to talking my mom into signing up as an officer and a nurse. We wound up at Ft. Bragg because our unit got called up for war duty, which meant April would be living without both mom and me for her senior year of high school.

All of these things were true, but I was not the reason things had turned out how they had. Thankfully, I came to realize that even in all this chaos, it wasn't my fault. Somehow, this was all going to work out, but I couldn't accept that at that moment.

Our family had come into contact with my father again, and he had harmed April. I was done with him. I was twenty-one years old. I had always longed to connect with my dad. And now this.

He was dead to me.

There was no hope for us anymore.

The MPs had arranged for my mother to stay behind to do what was necessary to protect April, and prosecute my father, but the Army decided I had to go. My grandparents took April home with them, and she lived with them while we were deployed. I was grateful to know she had them, but I was conflicted that I was not going to be there with her.

I would land in a war zone, not knowing what lay ahead of me, except what I had learned from training. And that wasn't enough to calm my nerves or settle my heart. Sitting on that long plane ride was the most difficult journey I have ever taken.

More Desert Reality

January, 17, 1991. Stepping off the plane in Saudi Arabia, I was welcomed by a surprise—rain! I didn't think it rained in the desert, but I would find out through experience that many things happen in the desert that are not expected.

We were placed in a huge warehouse; I think there were about a thousand troops packed in there. At least it felt that way. We were packed together for days, preparing for what was coming in the days ahead.

It wasn't too long before we met with our second desert reality. I kept a journal during our unit's deployment, and on January 17th, I wrote: "Woken up at 0100 hours. Told US is dropping first bomb at 0200, and we were expecting nerve gas."

Our First Sergeant walked up the steps to the barrack/warehouse, took out a Pre-nerve Agent tablet and consumed one. In an instant this communicated to all of us that we were about to start this war, and we were anticipating a chemical gas response. I took my first nerve agent pill with shaking hands. According to my journal, we took our second nerve agent pill at 0900. Things were about to get real.

The third desert reality—Scud Alarms.

There was this eerie, whining sound, and then a unified movement of humanity as all 1,000 soldiers scrambled to get gas masks and chemical suits on within mere seconds. That first scud alarm triggered the worst moment of my life as I realized I could die at any moment. There was no more time for training—this was for real. There were no guarantees about anything.

What if the pill doesn't work?
What if it does?

We had been told it would slow down the process of death if we did come into contact with chemicals, but it wasn't guaranteed to save us.

What if taking it now harms my health later on down the road?
What if I didn't make it out of here alive?

I immediately had thoughts about heaven. In that moment, my thoughts went immediately to what would happen if I were to die. I weighed my odds and figured I had an 80/20 chance of heaven versus hell. I was a pretty good person, and I went to church sometimes. That had to count for something, right? And I had just lived through the nightmare of my family reunion. Surely God would count that as a bonus on the good side of things.

I calmed myself with the idea that I had a pretty good chance of making it to heaven because I wasn't a terrible human. Little did I know that God was about to reveal His grace and show me just how wrong I was. I have since come to learn that going to church doesn't make you a Christian anymore than going to Steak 'n Shake makes you a cheeseburger. When you actually come face-to-face with imminent death, your perspective changes, and it changes quickly. I immediately began to think about what was important to me. Ironically enough, money didn't make the list.

This was just the first of many alarms in the desert. The attacks on our unit which caused the alarms would become so regular that we eventually started sleeping in our chemical suits and kept our gas masks within arm's reach. Each time we pulled off our protective gear, there would be a black charcoal-like residue on our skin. At first, we tried to wipe it off and get rid of any signs that we had used our gear. After a while, we didn't bother anymore. I settled into life in the barracks-like warehouse.

The fourth reality in the desert was how quickly my mom arrived. I thought she would spend some time in the States taking care of the issues with April, but the Army only gave her a few days to deal with what had transpired. Normally the process would have taken weeks if not months. But normal didn't exist here. We were at war.

Mom had to be strong for April, deal with the immense aftermath of what had happened, confront my dad, talk to the MPs, and then hand her daughter off to my grandparents as she got on a plane. My grandparents took care of April and would help her through the days ahead, and Mom arrived and joined our unit.

While I was glad to see her, I wished she wasn't there. I was so conflicted. I was grateful to have a familiar face with me in the desert, but I wanted her to be home with my sister, April. I wanted to know that both of them were safe.

The reality was that I was focusing a lot of energy on just taking care of myself in a war zone, and her arrival made me realize this was going to be even tougher than I thought. My new reality included being concerned about her well-being too.

It was another level of stress that I was not prepared for. But I learned to trust that she could take care of herself, and we were both going to be okay.

Gas Mask

As the days progressed through our time in the desert, we found a routine. At first, when the alarms would sound, we found ourselves all gravitating toward one wall of the warehouse. I am not sure what the thinking was—that particular wall was not any sturdier than the other three, but we gravitated together. Somehow, it made us feel safe in a dangerous environment, even though there was no truth that the wall would bring us any protection.

What *did* give us true protection was our gas masks. We had learned this in Basic Training. We were put in the gas chamber, had to do heavy calisthenics, and then take off our masks. We couldn't hold our breath due to all the exercises, so we breathed

deeply. Unfortunately, there was no perceived oxygen in the air. Of course, the Army wasn't going to kill us, but it felt like there was no air reaching our lungs! As we banged our fists on the wall in pure desperation, we all felt like we were going to die if we didn't get out.

We had to recite our social security number or weapon number before the Drill Sergeant would let us out. Once we were outside, everyone's eyes were watering and snot was hanging down to the ground from the effects. The purpose of this exercise was not to put us in harm's way, but to give us both head knowledge *and* heart knowledge that if we took care of our gas masks, our masks would take care of us.

On one of our convoys, a friend of mine dropped his mask on the desert road—if you could call the path we followed a *road*— we were barreling across in the desert. We did not stop. It was a sickening feeling knowing that he was as good as dead if we were attacked out there. I pondered the thought as we drove on.

What was I putting my trust in?

What gave me security?

The wall popped into my head.

Would that wall really hold up against an attack?

Just because people gather around a false belief doesn't make it true.

Why am I trusting in something that won't hold up against the attacks of life?

Our masks would work—the wall wouldn't. It started a thought process for me to re-evaluate all my mindsets.

Is there anything that will ever be secure enough to make me feel safe again?

How many times in life have I felt a false sense of security?

Just like that wall, or the pre-nerve pill for that matter, we think that something looks sturdy in our lives, but when the storms and the wars start, it literally will fall at our feet. Money? Success? Relationships? If we are depending on these to give our lives security, we are fooling ourselves, and there will be a moment when it all can come crashing down.

Birthday Cake, Not Really

We arrived in Kuwait and began to set up camp. One of our duties was to walk the area where we planned to set up camp and make sure there was nothing suspicious that could blow us up, so we all lined up and walked very slowly and cautiously through our future location where we would set up the Mobile Hospital.

Nerve wracking!

We were instructed to report anything that looked out of the ordinary. Once the area was cleared, camp set up began. The desert was massive—flat as far as the eye could see. The first evening there

34

it looked and felt like we were sitting on top of a huge birthday cake, and all I could do was look up and see what looked like huge candles around us. These *candles* were oil wells burning in the distance. They seemed to be less than a half mile away, but in actuality, they were several miles from us.

Our t-shirts would have oil stains on them by the end of the day because of all the oil that was in the air. The sandbags we used around our tents had oil droplets form on them throughout the day.

I wondered, *If I have kids, would they be born with three arms or two heads from all the toxins in the air over here?*

God has blessed us with four healthy children, and I am grateful that they challenge me to be a Godly parent, and that their antics do bring laughter to our home. But that part of the story comes much later down the road.

MASH stands for Mobile Army Surgical Hospital, and that meant we traveled around quite a bit in the desert.

Kuwait, Iraq, Bahrain, Saudi Arabia were all locations where we served during our stay in the desert. As you can imagine, traveling around in circles and not setting up camp for days or weeks, with no running water or a place to shower, we would stink, be tired and irritable, and long for the comforts of home. We had to do the best we could. There was a time period of grave danger, and mobilization, that we only had one shower in sixteen days. Yes, it was gross, but you would be surprised how quickly we grew accustomed to it. Everyone stank, and it very quickly became normal. That was life in the desert, in a war zone, and everyone just accepted it.

There were many things we had taken for granted before departing into the desert—toilets that flushed, washing hands in running water, taking a hot shower. We did the best we could to keep ourselves clean, but it's hard to stay clean in the desert sand and intense heat. Even the way we washed our clothes was strangely different in the desert.

Once we finally got a shower set up, we would line up to wash. In some remote places with tough conditions, our only option was to bring our clothes in the shower with us. While we took our turns, we put our clothes by our feet and let the water run off through our clothes. The soap we used on our bodies ran onto our clothes. Scrub for a few seconds, rinse, and *Voila*, our clothes were as clean as we were.

Sometimes, our *bathroom* facilities were PVC pipes in the ground with a little privacy around them. We just became accustomed to it and didn't question how to make it better.

When life throws things like war zones at us, it's time to stop and ask yourself, *What am I allowing myself to get accustomed to?*

The enemy of your soul will keep coming at you, perhaps through depression, guilt, anxiety, or loss of hope. It's easy to become accustomed to living with these dirty messes in our lives. I want you to know that it is okay to stop and question these things, and it is okay to get help.

None of us could make the situation in the desert better on our own, but together, we supported each other and tried to find ways to get through it. When we did make it through, we stopped using PVC pipes for urinals and showers for laundry. We didn't stay there, and you don't have to either.

Midnight Sheep

One of the most bizarre things I remember happening in the desert was midnight sheep.

We were in the middle of nowhere, and the only thing we could see at night were the huge fires off in the distance from the oil fields. With the exception of those fires, there was nothing to see—you could look 360 degrees around and all to be seen was flat, dry desert for what seemed like hundreds of miles.

We obviously tried to sleep at night, and some would joke about counting sheep. At midnight, we herd a commotion and jumped up to check our security. No humans in sight, but there was a herd of sheep that had wandered into our camp and were walking through, right by our tents.

We let the sheep pass on through, and they were safe from harm while they did. I never figured out where the sheep came from or why they were there, but looking back on it, I think God was trying to tell us that even sheep can survive in a war zone if they are in the right camp.

God calls us His sheep, and He makes sure that we make it through even the darkest nights and the hardest times when we are willing to walk into His camp and accept His security.

Mother's Day in the Desert

After my mom dealt with the fallout from the incident with my dad, she made her journey to the desert for her hospital assignment.

People have often asked me, "What's it like going to war with your mom?" or they might say, "It's neat you went to war with your mom." I have had a hard time putting it into words, but could you imagine how stressful it was to go to war, just myself, but then feel responsible for dragging my mother into a war zone as well? I felt like I needed to protect her, to take care of her and get us both out of there alive. She would say she didn't need my protection—but she's my mom!

While my mom was a nurse, my MOS (military occupation specialty) was 91MIKE—a hospital food service specialist. So not only did I feel responsible for my mom being in the war in the first place and believe I had to protect her, but I also was responsible as her main source of food! It was kind of fun to poke at her in the Mobile Kitchen Trailer line and remind her that I was paying her back for all those years of feeding me.

I was also my mom's inside connection for coffee—and she drank a lot of it in the desert. My mom wasn't the only coffee drinker in our unit. There were some who would pour the coffee packets into cold water just to have some caffeine.

It's always good to know the cook when you are at war, and Mom had the bonus of being family, not just another soldier. I saw her each day I worked as she passed through the Mobile Kitchen Trailer. Sometimes we worked every day in the kitchen, but once in a while we were able to rotate days off, so she got a little bit of a break from me, but not much.

One bright side to being deployed with my mother was that I did get to see her in person on Mother's Day. I was able to surprise her with a fresh cup of coffee and a hug. No one else in our unit was able to hug his or her mom that day. The small things became significant.

Another blessing in the desert was that my grandmother would always accept collect calls. We were able to call her on Mother's Day and wish her well. She and my grandfather also sent letters. Their words were so encouraging to us. I was always glad to hear her and my grandfather's voices on the phone, and I was so grateful that they took those calls, even knowing how much it cost them.

Those letters and calls were what helped keep us connected to home. I still have those letters, and the words are still precious as I remember the sacrifices they made to make sure we knew we were loved, even in the desert.

We cooked and served out of the MKT. After we had been in the desert for a while, people missed home and home cooked meals. There began to be some chatter about having the same things over and over. We did our best, but supply chain issues, as you can imagine, were a struggle.

One such item was the pop-top pasta meals. Kind of like SpaghettiOs, but Army style. To this day, my mother refuses to eat anything that resembles those meals in a can. There was a brief period of time where supply was really low, and there was a legitimate concern of when we were going to get our next shipment—just like that, the complaining stopped. Everyone became thankful to receive anything! We made sure their MREs were filling their stomachs, even when we couldn't do much about the other food supplies, and they appreciated how we tried to be creative with what we had and to make sure they were fed.

Their perspective changed when they realized how little we had. Little was better than nothing at all, and instead of complaining, they learned to compliment. Complimenting, even the small things, helps us all to be grateful—even in the desert with only beans and rice and pop-top pasta meals.

It is so important to be thankful for the little things, but don't wait until you have little before you start practicing gratitude. As a teenager, I learned from my mom's dad to appreciate the small things in life. When people complained about the weather, he would say, "Better than no weather at all." My grandfather taught me if there were no weather, we would be dead. My time in the desert helped me to remember that it's better to have something small than nothing at all.

I also learned that all sunshine makes a desert, so we need to be thankful for the rain. The things that we wouldn't necessarily choose for ourselves are the things that can help us grow. Trust me—I have been in the desert, and it's hot, and the sand gets into everything. You don't want to live there. We prayed for rain, and I was thankful for it.

Instead of complaining, consider offering a compliment and practicing gratitude. As Philippians 2:14 says, "Do everything without grumbling or arguing."

Friendships in the Desert

As our time in the desert continued, our unit set up in a compound, and we stopped moving around quite so much.

I learned some Arabic, and our group was assigned a translator. Her name was Reghed. She spoke English well, and she could translate the local Arabic dialects. She turned out to be a sweet woman with a great sense of humor considering the circumstances. Once we got to know her, we would spend time talking with her about life in Iraq. Even though she was a native, she thought Saddam Hussein was a madman—her words—and she wanted a better life for her people.

Reghed was afraid for her safety because she was helping us and did not know if she would be killed when she returned home. The thought crossed my mind to marry her, just to get her out of the desert and to the States and possibly save her life. Even in these difficult situations, she had a cheerful heart and hoped for a better day for herself and her people.

It broke my heart that she was sacrificing everything, maybe even her own life, to help us, but she was trying to help her people in the only way she knew. She opened my eyes to the ideas of helping our own. I know we were protecting the United States, even though we were miles from home, but she made me think about what I would do once I got back to the States.

Who could I help?

Where could I make a difference?

She challenged me to do more than just think about it. I hope

43

she is doing well. We lost touch after I came home, but the questions she posed and the example she set have not left me. Little did I know that those questions would be answered in some very interesting ways once my boots hit the dirt back home.

One of the ways I started to look around me was at the MASH. Now that we were in a compound, I was able to visit with the children at the hospital. Our unit had been assigned to a humanitarian mission, so we saw a lot of the people who had been hurt by the war. I tried to speak Arabic with some of the children, smile, and do silly things to try to make them laugh. Their smiles were priceless in the desert. To know that I was trying to lighten their loads, even for a moment, gave me some peace in my heart.

God used those little ones to spark a love in my heart that would eventually open my eyes to the Gospel and the invitation He was offering me through salvation by grace. The Bible says, "Let the little children come to Me," and I was learning why children were such a great example of faith. These children had survived a war, living in bad situations, had little or almost nothing, and had been injured by a fight they did not understand, yet they would smile and strike up friendships with us. They trusted us not to hurt them, but rather to look out for them and to be their friends.

In the same way, we may not understand everything going on around us, the world sometimes seems crazy and out of control, and yet we can trust Him to be our friend. He protects us, loves us, and builds a life for us that includes faith, joy, and hope. I started to see the darkness of the desert in my heart to disappear as I spent time helping in our MASH unit.

During one of our outings in Kuwait, I met an Egyptian boy who took me to his family's shop. I was checking out some of the neat things that were in the store, when the boy walked up to me with a water gun. He offered it to me, and I took off my hat and gestured it to him. We made a trade. He was very proud of his hat, and I liked my water gun, because it represented a connection I had made with this boy and his family.

They invited me to their home, and we shared a plate of fruit. It was a simple gesture, but it had a deeper meaning. These people were grateful for the military presence we had in their area. It helped to keep their lives stable and less chaotic, and they appreciated our being there. Sharing what they had and inviting us into their homes were ways that they expressed their gratitude for our service in their part of the world.

I was thankful that they wanted us there—so many others did not appreciate our presence and how we were trying to change the environment to help make their lives better, more stable, peaceful. This boy and his family shared what they had to let me know I was seen as a friend and not an enemy.

After I became a Christ follower, I learned how important it is that we portray ourselves as allies, not enemies, to a lost world. We will not win anyone to the kingdom with bravado and pride. But when we dig into the trenches with them, when we protect them with our prayers, and when we are willing to stand with them for what is right and good, then we earn the right to be respected. We will then be invited to join them, and they will share what their lives are like with us, and connections occur. Connections lead to relationships, and those relationships give us the opportunity to introduce them to Jesus.

All because I was willing to give up a hat, I gained a friendship. It wasn't my plan to go to the desert to make friends. Philippians 2:3–5 tells us that we should look after the interests of others and put others needs above our own. Am I serving others by being friendly and giving the opportunity for a friendship to grow, even if it's with someone who is very different from me?

The desert friendships were not my plan, but they were part of God's, and He does such a better job of leading us to the people we need.

Things were always a little chaotic in the desert, but there were certain things that were real messes.

I told my boss to take a day off, and I would cover breakfast for him. My boss, Barry, was a great guy with a great sense of humor and an impressive work ethic. He told the joke that his mom had twins and Tripletts at the same time. Barry actually had a twin brother named Harry, and their last name was Triplett. His attitude and good humor made working in the Mobile Kitchen Trailer much easier. He didn't let things get him down, and he didn't complain.

He had been working a lot of shifts, and I wanted to help him out, so he took me up on the offer. The only problem was, somehow some fuel had leaked from an M2 burner—and I set the Mobile Kitchen Trailer on fire!

I didn't mean to. Things just got out of hand because of that fuel leak, and a fire broke out. It was so bad we had to shut down breakfast. I felt terrible about the whole thing, and I was working as hard as I could to clean up the mess when my boss, Barry Triplett, walked in. He had heard the commotion and found out about the fire.

One of the things that always stuck out to me was how he responded. Barry just picked up a towel and jumped in to help me clean up. He was so gracious during the whole clean up, and he never once yelled at me. We worked hard and were able to be back open for lunch. His example of kindness under pressure was a great lesson for me. Barry was a great guy, but that day, he became a giant in my book. He didn't show any anger, and he helped me clean up the huge mess I made that day.

Barry passed away in 2017. I was sorry to hear of his passing. His gracious spirit and lack of anger showed me how much God's presence could change a person. I would not have responded the way Barry did. To this day I still remember his example.

Because of his gracious kindness, I learned that we do not have to berate people when they have made mistakes. They are probably already beating themselves up in their own heads, and we can make a much greater impact on their lives if we just pick up the towel and help them clean up the mess.

I saw that day that God isn't up in the heavens with a huge baseball bat waiting to beat me over the head the first—or second, or millionth—time I messed up. Like Barry, God is willing to jump in and help clean up the mess.

DEPLOYED WITH MY MOTHER

An encouraging verse to me is Romans 8.28. Even though we mess up at times, and sometimes bad things happen to good people, God can take every situation, and in ways we don't understand or fathom, somehow use that for the good of those who love Him.

A quote I really like and lean on at times is, "No good sea captain was made on calm seas." The only way a captain can help navigate others to safety is through the trials and tribulations he has faced and overcome. Sometimes it is better to weather the storm and come through it instead of running from it. We can use our difficult past experiences to help others if we allow God to work through us.

Another mess that we had to contend with in the desert was, well—poop. Because we were in the desert, and we were a mobile unit, our latrines were set up to flow into large metal containers, and we would have to burn the human excrement to keep our camps and compounds sanitary.

Many of us were assigned to *poop detail*. We would pour fuel into the container to help with the ignition, and then we would light the fecal matter. Poop detail required that we stir the sludge down until all of it was burned. Eww, it was gross, but it was necessary.

There will be times when God removes the stink in our lives when we are obedient and repentant of our sin. Maybe it's a sin that has to be burned out of our thinking or actions, or maybe it's an attitude that has to go to help our lives become cleaner.

Poop stinks when it is left to sit, and sin is the same way in our spirits. I would come to learn, as unpleasant as it is in the moment, it is always best to burn the crap in our lives. Physically in the desert, we burned it; spiritually in our hearts, God has to change us. Neither is a pleasant assignment, but both are necessary to keep the stench of sin, or crap, from overrunning our camp.

In addition to my kitchen duties, I also worked convoy duty. I drove a big 2 ½ ton truck, called a deuce-and-a-half.

Since we were a MASH unit, and the "M" stands for Mobile, we had to move our unit regularly. During these travels in the desert, we sometimes didn't know where we would end up for the night. Therefore, each one of us was on our own to find a place to sleep when we stopped. Because I was a driver of one of the trucks, I would save a spot for my mom to sleep underneath my truck—an added bonus for me being in the desert with my mom. At least I could provide a safe place for her to sleep.

One intense moment came at night while driving under cover. Naturally, one does not use headlights when driving in Iraq at night in the middle of war. We drove our trucks using little reflectors on the front and back of our vehicles for guidance.

Our First Sergeant ordered my truck forward with a, "Go, Go!" command. I floored my deuce-and-a-half as the vehicle in front of me had gotten too far ahead to see the reflectors. I was driving thirty to thirty-five miles per hour, and I could see nothing in front of me. I was driving blind in complete pitch blackness. I had to constantly remind myself of the truth and debunk all the lies that were filling my head.

There are no ditches, no light poles, no oncoming traffic because I am in the middle of the desert. I won't run into anything, except possibly the truck in front of me, assuming it was still way ahead.

If I had let any of those lies into my mind, or acted on them, I would have been paralyzed and would not have been able to carry out the mission my First Sergeant had given. My fingers were white from gripping the steering wheel so hard. My heart was racing a mile a minute. Eventually, I caught up with the rest of the convoy, and my heart rate started to slowly return to normal.

We made it to our destination because I refused to give into the fear that was trying to blur my vision. Fear tried to derail me from my mission and could have caused a delayed or failed mission if I had let it take control of my mind.

It is the same in life—we have to know the truth and act on it. If we let lies creep in, we lose our ability to focus, and we will get derailed.

Driving in the darkness taught me to appreciate the light. It is so much easier to drive when you have lights! It is a good reminder to walk in the light, because that is where Jesus is, and because that is where the path is easier to see.

Cruise Boat

After spending what seemed like an eternity in the desert, our unit was chosen to enjoy some time on a cruise ship.

We were notified that we would have an opportunity to go on the boat, but we were not sure when it would happen. Knowing it was coming made enduring the misery of daily life in the desert more bearable. Doing without the basics for even a few months was tough. Not knowing when it would end made it tougher.

The day came, and it was finally the 912th's chosen time to enjoy the cruise. Living in the desert without having a sink where you can turn a handle and have water come out, not having a toilet that flushes, or even a shower with a knob that turns on the hot water was harder than most people understand. It was difficult to go without running water for so long, and it wore on the morale of our group as time dragged on in the desert.

This ship was a luxury cruise liner with all the attractions. There was good food, drinks, and even a karaoke stage. Having spent months in the desert, this ship seemed like a piece of heaven. The simplest things, such as running water, were awesome. I felt like a little kid once I got into my room on the ship. I turned the sink handle and watched the water come out. I flushed a toilet and took a shower by simply turning on the faucet. Running water was awesome!

I swam in the pool, ate things I hadn't seen in months, tried new foods for the first time in my life—and that karaoke stage? I managed to talk one of the dancers into letting us borrow her gloves so we could perform. We needed the gloves because my buddy, David Oakley, and I sang a masterpiece, with loud voices and lots of gusto. Michael Jackson's "Beat It" would never sound the same after that day! I am so grateful that iPhones were not a thing during our time in the desert. Recordings of that day would have been embarrassing now, but it was a great time of joy on a cruise ship after living in the desert for months.

There's a story in the Bible of Jesus celebrating a wedding feast with His countrymen. He interrupted funerals and caused there to be joy. He raised the dead to give others hope. Those few days on that ship helped to revive our morale and give us the encouragement to persevere.

We came back renewed and refreshed, and for a while, the desert wasn't quite so bad. The time on the cruise ship had breathed life back into us again. It was the same sun beating down on us, but we felt its heat differently, and the compound routine wasn't quite so monotonous.

In my journey to find Jesus as Lord, I have learned that He gives rest and renews our spirits, but we have to be willing to take the R&R and step onto the boat He has waiting for us. Otherwise, we will burn ourselves out and be bored with our routine, all because we wouldn't take a step of change.

I also learned not to take the little things for granted, but to be grateful for it all. After having gone without running water, even though it was a brief period of time compared to eternity, it was long enough to remind me that a grateful heart recognizes even the smallest of blessings and gives God glory for so personally meeting our needs.

I learned to be grateful for the rest, and I learned to be thankful for the desert too.

Graduation

We had been in the desert for about five months. We had moved countless times. We would set up camp, take care of the injured and sick, break down camp, drive through the desert and start the process all over again.

With the war winding down, there were fewer injured, and the Army decided that we had completed our mission. The Army also determined that all but sixty or so of our unit would return home.

But, this was the Army, so it seemed like word changed on a daily basis. One day we were told we would be going, the next day we were told we would be staying. There were rumors of pullout dates and then we would hear of cancellation dates. It was nuts.

It was close to April's graduation, so I was hoping against hope that Mom would be able to get out of the desert and be back in time to see my sister walk across the stage and get her diploma. But it was the same song and dance.

Mom got the word, "Yes, you will make it for graduation."

The next day, "Nope, doesn't look like it's going to work out."

"Oh wait...maybe we can work it out after all."

Anyone who has ever served in the military knows everything is subject to change. It was an up and down, emotional rollercoaster, so we decided not to tell April what was going on, because we didn't want to get her hopes up and then disappoint her.

Mom and I kept it between us. Each day we talked about it—hoping at least one of us would get to be there for graduation. I hoped it would be Mom, and I think she secretly hoped it would be her too.

53

Finally, it was determined that Mom would not get home in time for graduation, and I was going to be part of the drawdown unit, so it was a no-go for me too.

We were crushed. All our hopes and plans crumbled with three simple words: *not this time.* I struggled once again because I had talked Mom into signing up, and she was going to miss something really important again because of our tour in the desert. We didn't have the heart to call home and tell April. We struggled to stay positive with each other, and we knew that a phone call home would reveal our disappointment.

But wait! Things changed again.

The main unit was slated to leave from Khobar Towers at 03:20 on the 6th of June and arrive at Fort Bragg at 5 PM. My mom arranged special transportation from Ft. Bragg to make it to graduation, which was at 7 PM—a measly two-hour window.

Our cousin David was going to be waiting and would take her straight to Fayetteville Airport where our neighbor Cliff (who worked for Moody Aviation) would be waiting to take her in a plane and fly her to east Tennessee.

Then word came that the flight was delayed until 11:30 the morning of the 7th of June, and Mom was disappointed to the core. She called to cancel the arrangements that were just made.

Plans were then made to have Heather's mom, Cheri, video the graduation—not the same as being there, but still thankful to be heading home. Mom then took a taxi to King Abdulaziz airport to check the manifest for the day to see if she could possibly fly out with another unit and maybe make the graduation.

There was a plane leaving at 10 AM for Philadelphia. She spoke with many people at the terminal and with customs and finally located a DD1610—a necessary form for travel. In the process of getting back to the unit, she had to hitchhike and then finally got in a taxicab. The driver's English was terrible. He pulled over and picked up two more people.

Sensing something was off, one of them said they could help my mom get where she wanted to go. It turned out the driver didn't have a clue where she was going. She made it back. She informed the major of her findings about the manifest and that there was a vacancy on the plane, and he signed the form.

It was all hands-on deck at this point. Several people jumped in and helped her get ready. She surrendered her weapon, and they helped carry her bags down the stairs and made a contact for her to get a ride to the airport. Sergeant Patillo escorted her to the airport. She stopped at the terminal, got her form stamped, went to the customs terminal, walked through the amnesty booth, got briefed, and then everything in her purse was examined.

Thankfully, they did not have to open her other bags which were jam-packed full. The Military Police carried her baggage to the plane, and within a few minutes the plane was airborne.

Mom was shocked it went up so quickly, but once the plane was in the air, everybody started clapping. She was on the way to Philadelphia.

Mom still had no idea how she was going to get to Tennessee, but once she landed, she checked with the ticket agents and found that she could get a ride to Cincinnati that day and then from Cincinnati to Tri-Cities Airport which would arrive about 5 PM. She called my grandmother, who was at work, and asked her if she could pick her up at the airport.

My grandparents picked her up at the terminal, took her to the nearest beauty shop to get her hair trimmed, stopped for a bite to eat, and finally delivered her to the high school in time for the graduation ceremony.

April had no idea that Mom was going to be there. She was in a room with her classmates getting ready. Mom still vividly remembers walking into the room and seeing her. It was one of the happiest moments of her life.

April graduated that day with the biggest smile on her face. My mom won the award for traveling the farthest to attend graduation. She even got her picture in the local newspaper as her reunion with April on Graduation day was front-page news. My name was printed in the article along with a small blurb about how I had to stay back in the desert, but April and Mom got the reunion of the lifetime.

They spent a month together talking, reuniting, and getting used to being back together again. Mom adjusted back to civilian life, and the two of them were inseparable during that time. It was hard not to be jealous, but I knew my mom and sister needed this time to reconnect. I was just glad Mom made it back and that she was able to be present and celebrate with April for her graduation. I wouldn't have traded those moments for anything for them. I just felt like a big piece of me was very far away during this time, and I wanted to belong somewhere.

I realize the military's *subject to change* policy is the world's system. The world often makes promises it can't deliver—it can make you crazy with the never-ending ups and downs and uncertainties if you let it.

God's way is not like that. God has a will and a purpose that started before the world began. He never loses control of anything in this life and the next, and He always holds His children in His hand. God promises peace, and He delivers—just like He delivered my mom back to the States in time for April's graduation.

God has a plan, and His plan brings peace and promises that cannot be broken.

Munition's Dump

After my mom and the majority of my unit left for the States, I stayed behind with about sixty other soldiers to finish our mission as the rear detachment—a small group left behind to close down operations.

Mom had seen the ravages of the war in the MASH unit, and while she was glad to be home, she knew I was still there. We were able to talk on the phone, and one particular call left my mother in complete fear. As I was talking with her on the phone around 11 AM on July 11, 1991, there was a loud explosion. Walls trembled and glass started shattering. The last thing I said was, "Holy...." and hung up the phone.

Can you imagine my mother's reaction when she heard the explosion and my response? She wrote in her journal that she immediately wondered if I was okay. Was I still alive, or had one of her worst nightmares come true? She was worried sick.

I ran outside the warehouse. There were explosions and smoke everywhere. We were under attack! It was raining shrapnel, and stuff was on fire. My heart raced and I could not find my unit.

What is my next step?

I need to get to safety, but where should I go?

How did a poor kid, who signed up to be a cook for a reserve unit in the hills of Tennessee—just so he could get some money to pay for college—wind up running through the desert, surrounded by black smoke as he tried to make his way to safety? After what seemed like an eternity, I found a safety zone with another unit of random people I did not know, and I stayed with them for several hours while the explosions kept going on and on.

Things were still exploding, and there was black, thick smoke everywhere when we finally got word that we are not under attack. It turns out the munition dump had ignited. Vehicles, tanks, and weapons had caught fire and were exploding, and there was no safe route out, so we hunkered down to wait it out.

Hours later, we finally got the all clear. The whole day had been spent in a safety zone. I finally located my unit and went in the building. I started seeing familiar faces, then something strange happened. Everyone was excited to see me.

I was stunned at their reaction—why the big welcome back? Why were people so excited to see me? Why were they acting like I was some celebrity to be paraded into camp?

Apparently, it's a big deal when you make it back to camp when you are MIA—missing in action. I didn't even know I was considered missing!

The unit had done a head count after the munition dump exploded, communication gear had gone silent—the phone call with my mom had gone dead for that reason—and I was detoured to wait it out. That detour took me eight hours, and when the unit hadn't been able to find me after the initial explosion, I was labeled MIA. I found out later that my picture had even shown up on the evening news in my hometown, and everyone there was worried about me, fearing the worst. My mom was interviewed by the television journalist near our hometown, and she had told them about the moment just before the phone had gone dead.

According to the *Johnson City Press*, 11 July 1991: "Ammo Depot Explodes at U.S. Base: An explosion ripped through a U.S. ammunition depot Thursday showering soldiers with shells and shrapnel and engulfing vehicles in flames. The chain reaction blast at the Black Horse Camp in Doha apparently began with an electrical fire on a truck carrying 155 howitzer shells. We have lost more tanks today than we did in the whole war. It was blowing out shrapnel so we had to pull back and then boom it went off. The Black Horse Camp is a last major contingent of U.S. troops in Kuwait."

My mindset had been determination to get back to my camp, my brothers and sisters at arms, and to sleep on my own cot that night. The thought had not even occurred to me that someone would be looking for me. The moment I realized my unit thought I was gone, thought the worst had happened but didn't want to believe it, and then they celebrated when I returned—it blew my mind.

Later in life, I realized this is what Jesus and fellow believers must feel like when a person bows the knee to the Savior and returns home—truly home to their spiritual family.

So many times in life, we think we need to go it alone, there is radio silence as we shut ourselves off from those who are looking for us—the same ones who celebrate when we've been found. Too many times, the dark smoke of depression, the hazards of isolation and fear, all send us on a detour in life. We are choking as we try to breathe through dark moments, and all that time, Someone keeps the light on and is watching, waiting for us.

We must find our way ourselves in order to realize that we were lost. That day, the power of God revealed peace in my heart. There was always going to be a family to come home to. I didn't put it all together in that moment, but there is always Someone who is searching for me, and He is not going to allow me to remain Missing in Action. There was Someone who didn't care how much money I had, or how successful I was going to be in life. He was there. And He had His own army of believers who were going to make sure I didn't do life alone.

This poor kid, turned reservist cook, had just found the most valuable treasure in all of life—belonging. Looking back now, this was the moment that my life changed; my mindset got flipped over on its own head. These fellow soldiers did not reach into my pockets to see how much money I had—they were thankful I was alive. They were grateful I had made it back, and they were genuinely glad to see me.

I had found relationship, belonging, and companionship within this unit that I had never known outside of the relationship with my mom. When the ruckus had finally settled down in camp, I went to my tent, got showered, and then sat on the end of my bunk for a while.

I called my mom again and told her I was okay. As a child, I had walked through the snow, been put in a truck with a stranger and was protected by my then-unknown Savior. As an adult, I had walked through the sand in the desert, sheltered with a unit of strangers, and was still protected by my unknown Savior. Though I did not know Him personally yet, there was a God who had protected us, and I felt hope in my heart. I was going to make it through this desert, and I was finding new treasures along the way.

Nothing could change the fact that God had taken me to the desert to find Him. He had to use a war zone to break my mindset. Things were going to be different from here on out, and I would have to choose to keep moving forward. It would be a while before I totally understood what surrender to a Savior meant and how that was the most important decision I would need to make. But for now, I was moving with two sets of boot prints—not just mine, but His too. He was going to work things out in my life. I would come face-to-face with the reality that He loved me and didn't want me to be MIA from His kingdom.

As you read this, maybe you find yourself in the blizzard or the desert. You don't have to wait until you figure it all out, until you understand it all. Just know, this is *your* moment—your moment to know that Jesus Christ loves you so much that He went to Calvary and died in your place. He is searching for you, and you don't have to be MIA from His kingdom any longer.

Ask Him to be Your hope, to rescue you from whatever is holding you captive, and know that the Savior is waiting with open arms to welcome you home.

Going Home, or Maybe Not

In order to close down camp, we had to get rid of stuff. We packed up equipment and shipped it back stateside, we did more poop burning duty, and then the order came to burn the tents.

Burning the tents meant we would no longer have shelter or protection from the desert weather. It meant the final steps were being made for us to get out of the desert. We piled the tents up, added a little fire incentive to get the flames going, and then we stood back and watched.

Reality set in. That fire meant we were done. Flames were going up, and we were going home.

The 912th MASH unit had completed its mission, and we were finished.

We had survived.

We had made it through the desert.

We had survived the war.

And we were truly going home.

The desert was no longer our place, no longer the home-away-from-home, no matter how uncomfortable it had been. Shortly after the fire was out, we picked up our packs and headed for the trucks. The trucks took us to the airport, and the airport staff led us to a plane— if you could call it a plane.

I thought, *I just survived a war in the desert, and I am going to die trying to get home.*

The plane was named *Sun Country*. I had never heard of this airline, and I am pretty sure no one else on the plane had either.

Why couldn't it have been a Delta plane? Or even Qatar Airlines? Why did it have to be Sun Country? We boarded anyway. We made the bumpy trip to Germany, and from Germany we flew all night to Ft. Bragg. Sun Country did a fine job after all, and I was thankful.

Once at Ft. Bragg, we worked our way through processing and debriefing. Then, it was time to go home. I stood outside the base and took a moment to take it all in. I didn't realize it then, but I see it now—the Lord had watched over every step I had taken in the desert. He brought me safely back and had done the same for Mom too. As I rode the bus home, one of the most impactful and memorable sights was seeing fire trucks with big American flags draped across the ladders as we rode back into town. This memory is engraved in my mind, and sticks with me even today. A sense of great patriotism swelled inside me as we drove by those flags.

When we got to Johnson City, people were cheering and waving. I had not signed up for the Reserves because of my great patriotism—I had signed up to help pay for school—but my time in the desert had shown me a great appreciation for the freedoms and rights being an American brings, and my time there had changed my heart. I felt a sense of pride. I had been a part of something bigger than myself that had brought honor to my country. I was overwhelmed by the encouragement and support from afar—so many strangers standing on the curbside, cheering us home. I took a moment to stop and think of all the veterans who had come before me—some weren't welcomed home like this. I bowed my head and gave a moment of respect for each one of them. They deserved this too, and I wanted to extend that gratitude to them at that moment.

When the bus pulled into the 912th MASH parking lot, my whole family, Heather and her family, and a great group of friends were waiting for us to disembark. It was incredible! There was no better feeling in the world than to be surrounded by loved ones who were so happy to have me home. Mom, April, my grandparents and so many others were there. We celebrated right there in the parking lot!

From there, we went to see my Great Granny, and I had the opportunity to show her my medals and tell her the stories from the desert. Granny loved to hear the stories, and she beamed with pride and respect as she handled my medals. She was gracious and kind, and it is one of my favorite memories. We even took pictures together. She smiled ear to ear. Having her picture taken with her *war hero* great-grandson was a big deal to her, and an etched moment in time I will not forget. I am so glad I had those moments with her, and I treasure those memories.

Those moments were more important to me than any medals I could have ever gotten in the desert. I was realizing that belonging to a family, showing unconditional love, and blessing others with encouragement were all medals I could bestow on the ones I love, and they are far more valuable than any tangible thing the world offers.

The Breakup

It was so good to be with Heather again after I came back to the States! I really liked spending time with her, and she had been such an encouragement to me through her faithfulness, letters, packages, and the love she shared with me while I was deployed.

Her steadiness helped me to avoid a lot of funny business, regrets, and relationship dangers while I was deployed, because I knew she was waiting for me back home. I will always be grateful for all she and her family were to me and my mom through that season of life.

Heather and I both realized over time, however, that our romantic relationship was not part of God's long-term plan for us. The trust we had developed, and the friendship that we cultivated allowed us to continue to stay friends, even after we decided to end the romantic part of the relationship. Our families would still get together for picnics and celebrations, and the friendship that continued between our families was a great blessing.

Heather eventually joined the military, and she met a wonderful soldier who was the right one for her. I met my wife, Trish, a little while later, and I am forever grateful that the Lord knows what is truly best, and that He led both me and Heather to the spouses He had planned for us.

I think it is important to value the friendships and relationships God allows in our lives and to not take people for granted. I know that separation can be difficult, whether it is a deployment or a decision that changes the relationship, but it is important that we live with integrity and trust so we don't damage the relationships God gives us. And we should also find peace in the knowledge that God does all things well, and He will lead us to the lifetime relationships we should have when we follow Him. He doesn't ever take something away without giving us something better, because He is a good Father and a great God. He sees the end from the beginning, and He knows who we need in each season of our lives to strengthen our character, to know true friendship, and to be loved unconditionally.

Letters were such an important part of my journey in the desert. Knowing that family and friends, and sometimes even strangers, were thinking of us and took the time to write to us was a great encouragement.

Mail call was a special time in Basic Training and also in the desert. Everyone loved getting personal letters or packages. I received letters from my family, my girlfriend, and friends. It really helped me to cope with the situation at hand, and the letters took my mind off of the war, even if it was only for a few moments. We were also fortunate to receive letters from strangers. In my journal, I had written down the times I received letters, and I remember one letter that really impacted me was from Elias Mendoza (thank you, Elias!). It was a letter to *any service member*, but he was very grateful for our service, and his words stuck with me on the battlefield.

One regret I have is that I have lost some of the letters that were written to *any service member*, and I do not have a way to write them back now. Those letters meant so much in the desert, and I would love to tell those individuals how much I appreciated it then and now.

I currently have letters from Desert Storm that I have not opened yet. Yes, you read that correctly. The reason I haven't read the letters is that I received them after I got home from the desert. I was glad to receive the letters, I decided I wanted to keep them and save them to read later. I put them in a special place in my room, but I didn't open them. I know you are thinking, *You must be crazy!*

Those letters are from family, and they wanted you to know they love you and how much they care about you.

Those letters are over 30 years old. But at the time I thought, *I have all the time in the world to read those now.* And I set them aside and never read them.

In the same way, each of us has a letter written to us, and many of us have set it aside, maybe even in a special place, but we haven't taken the time to read it. This is a love letter from God.

You may think you know what it says. Some are not the least bit interested, and others have a misunderstanding of what they *think* it says, because they have never read it. I am talking about the Scriptures, the Bible, the love letter from God—and if you haven't read your letter from God, you are crazier than I am for not reading my letters.

The Bible gives us hope and encouragement, whether we are in the desert or in the comfort of our own homes. You might think you have plenty of time to read what God says. Or perhaps it's just not a high priority right now. But you couldn't be further from the truth.

In the desert, those letters were a lifeline. But when I got home, I didn't treasure or appreciate them as I should have. That is one of my biggest regrets. I also regret that I lost Elias' letter and never had the opportunity to write him back and thank him for taking the time to write and tell him how much I appreciated it. I didn't keep those letters from the desert, and I have wished many times that I could have written back to those people and thanked them.

God's Word, God's *love letter*, is our lifeline. Treasure it. Hold onto it. Appreciate the encouragement and love that God put into it instead of setting it on a shelf and promising that you'll get around to reading it someday.

I have a desire to know what is in those unopened letters, but my prayer is that I desire to know God's Word even more than what is in those earthly letters.

Perhaps I need to go read them now.

East Tennessee State University

The summer after I graduated from high school, a recruiter called, and the next thing I knew, I was signing on the dotted line and being sworn in to the United States Army.

Before Basic Training, I signed up for a semester of general classes at ETSU. I shipped off to Basic in December. I came back and took a few more semesters of school before we shipped out in 1990. Looking back on those times when I was in school, I realized I would get really stressed and worried about taking tests.

One day in the desert I thought about those stressful moments, and I just had to chuckle at myself. All that worry and stress over a test.

Now my tests were daily survival skills, and I made a vow to myself that day in the desert that when I made it home, I was going back to school, and I was going to keep it all in perspective. If I failed a test or missed a day of class, at least I knew I wouldn't die because of it. The worst that could happen would be that I would get a C or possibly have to retake the course. No big deal. At least I would be alive to take it again.

So many of my perspectives changed through the course of my ordeals in the desert. This new perspective gave me hope that I would survive, I would go back to school, and I would persevere to reach that goal. And I would do it without so much worry.

Even now when things are not going according to my plan, I think back and say, "Hey, this is just a test. At least I'm not getting shot at. This problem is not nerve gas or an enemy sniper."

We are all going to have moments in life when we feel like things are at their worst, and it is never going to get better—but that is a lie. Circumstances do change, life does get better, and we should hang onto hope and count our blessings instead of our problems. It helps to keep us in a positive frame of mind and gives us the determination to keep moving forward.

I took the first semester of college off after I returned from the desert. I was still living with Mom, and we continued to help each other adjust. We both found humor to help us get through some of the dark thoughts that would creep in now and then, and it was good to have someone who understood—who had been there—to talk through it.

I was ready to start back in the spring of 1992, and I re-enrolled. When our unit had been activated, I had to drop all classes immediately, so when I did reenroll, I was taking the same exact classes I had dropped.

One of those classes was Economics, and I distinctly remember the first day of class after I came back from war. My Economics teacher was taking role, but paused when he got to my name. He had this perplexed look on his face.

"Are you the David Weill that had to drop my class because of Desert Storm?"

"Yes, sir."

He stopped and thanked me for my service and said was glad to have me back, right there in front of the entire class. It impressed me so much that he recognized me and gave me that shout out in front of my classmates. It felt good to be appreciated, and I still remember that moment even thirty years later. It was a small gesture, but it had a huge impact.

In life, we need to remember that it is the little things that we can do for others—making them feel appreciated, doing small things that show them we value them—that can make an impact long-term in their lives, and possibly ours too.

I remember my English teacher allowed me to submit some

work that I had done at Ft. Bragg before we left, and she gave me credit for that class, which was an added blessing, so I didn't have to take English while trying to adjust back to college life. I crammed four years of school into seven—including Basic Training and my time in the desert—so every credit, every blessing, helped.

My teachers were appreciative of my service, but they didn't allow me to slide on any requirements. I was held to the same standards as the other students. I appreciated that. Knowing I had to make the grades the same as everyone else, that there was a standard for me to live up to, built my confidence in my ability to study, learn, and grow.

Having survived the biggest test of my life—from potential chemical weapons to exploding munitions piles—a paper test did not have the power to rattle me anymore. I found that I was much more willing to accept a challenge academically, knowing that it wouldn't be able to kill me, and I spent my last three years in school devoted to accomplishing my goal.

My mom was one of my biggest cheerleaders during my school journey. When I got discouraged, she would say, "Remember the desert. What doesn't kill you makes you strong. You are stronger than you ever thought possible."

She was right. But there was still something missing in my life. The accomplishments, the good grades, it was all good—but it still didn't fill that void in my heart.

While I was in college at East Tennessee State University, someone invited me to a meeting with Campus Crusade for Christ—now known as CRU. I wish I could remember who the person was, but I just remember being invited and having a lot of fun, surrounded by good people. I enjoyed the meetings and I felt like I fit in with this group.

They offered summer mission trips, called Summer Projects, and I decided to go. There was an application to fill out—we told about ourselves, why we wanted to go on the trip, etc. I stated that I was a Christian, and the reason I thought I was one was because I went to church, and I was trying to be a good person. I was accepted by the team leadership and went to Daytona Beach during the summer of 1993.

Earle Chute and his lovely wife, Cara, were the directors of the trip. They have spent countless years investing in the lives of college students and making a difference in untold hundreds, if not thousands, of lives. While there, I was in a small group, had a job at the Aladdin Inn, and was surrounded by Godly men and women who were living out their faith. It was like being in a greenhouse environment—my faith was being planted, prepped, and ready to burst into full bloom. I just didn't know it—until training night.

While we were being trained in different methods of sharing our faith, it occurred to me that being a *good* person and going to church no more made me a Christian than going to Steak 'n Shake makes someone a cheeseburger.

We learned verses like Romans 3:23—*For all have sinned and fall short of the glory of God*; Romans 6:23—*For the wages of sin is death, but the gift of God is eternal life through Jesus Christ our Lord.* And I realized I was a sinner and that I was separated from God because of my sin. It became crystal clear to me that Jesus Christ, being God Himself, died on the cross so that I could have the option to be forgiven of my sin. I repented and gave my life to God through what Christ had done for me on the cross.

I really struggled with the truth of the Gospel. After all, I had learned to be resourceful and determined. I had a *do-it-on-your-own* attitude. But Ephesians 2:8–9 says God's salvation is a gift. It took another shift in my mindset to realize that I was in bondage. It was like I was handcuffed by the old sinful man I was, but I couldn't realize it. I had lived handcuffed for so long, I thought this was the normal way to live.

But once I learned the truth, I wanted the cuffs off! I tried to get them off myself, to turn over a new leaf, to be a better person, to go to church more regularly—all to try to rid myself of the guilt that came with being a sinner.

But, that's not God's way. To be freed from bondage, the Master has to set you free. Jesus came to do this for us! Out of His great love, He came to earth, lived a sinless life, died as our sinless sacrifice, and then rose from the grave to prove that He is God and there is no other. He offers freedom—true freedom—as a gift. We can't work for it, earn it, or pay our own way for it. We simply have to accept it.

The moment I bowed my knee in surrender to the God of the universe, to the Savior of my soul, was the moment those shackles fell off. Before surrender, I thought I would be fine. After hearing all of this, understanding it is a gift from God Himself, I gave my life to Christ and decided to live for Him—not for money, not for self, but for Him and His glory.

He came in and set up camp in my heart, and my desire is that He be in charge and lead and guide me the rest of my days. Little did I know then, but the time I had spent in the desert had brought me to this moment, and I was going to learn that every lesson, every step during my time in the desert was valuable. I was going to move forward in every area of life, and Jesus was going to change me.

Thankfully, He is patient and loving and kind, but every lesson from the desert would come back to play out in my life here in the States. My life was changed that summer as I became a child of God. Being forgiven is a priceless gift, and I had just received it—while training to take the message of God's gift to others.

I was embarrassed that I had thought all this time that I was a Christian, and I didn't tell anyone what had happened that night. However, God still used that summer in my life as I grew like a plant in a greenhouse and experienced God's love and forgiveness.

It wasn't until a year or so later, while back on campus at East Tennessee State University, that Earle asked me to give my testimony at one of our meetings.

I distinctly remember sitting outside on the concrete floor thinking, *Which testimony should I give, the one where I thought I was a Christian, or the true story of what God revealed to me about my lost state while on a missions trip?*

I still hadn't told anyone about my actual conversion experience, because that would have required me to be vulnerable. I made my decision.

I started my testimony that night by saying, "I'm going to tell you all something that I have never told anyone in my life."

I remember Earle sitting on the edge of his seat throughout my story. I told the truth of thinking I was alright because I was a decent person, a good person, but that wasn't enough. I told how sitting there that night at training, learning the verses, and understanding that the Gospel was for me—that Jesus died because He loved me—the joy and the relief of releasing that burden was incredible. I learned then and there to never be ashamed of how God had worked in my life.

"We are all on different journeys," I told them. "And all our stories bring glory to Him when we are willing to share them."

Earle continued to work with me, and I eventually shared with him all the bitterness and anger I had toward my dad for what he had done—and *not* done—in my life. Earle taught me that bitterness is a poison pill I take, hoping the other person will die. He helped me understand God's forgiveness, grace, and mercy. Because of Earle's non-judgmental attitude, his gracious sharing of God's Word, and his loving way of speaking truth into my life, I began the process of healing. God used Earle's influence in my life to teach me that holding onto bitterness, rage, and anger was not going to give me the life I envisioned.

I had the daunting task of trying to forgive my father—of finding peace when I knew he would never apologize or ask for forgiveness.

While I was growing up, Mom did everything she could to help fill the void that my dad left by being there for us, letting me have a Big Brother mentor, Dennis White, who spent time with me and was there for me—even though I did lose contact with him as an adult—and allowing good men to speak truth into my life. But she wasn't able to help me at this point, because we each had to deal with our own bitterness and anger, and mine had built up over time like water behind a dam. There was so much pain and hurt that I was going to have to deal with, but God brought it all to a breaking point. Forgiving my dad was my own personal journey because it was my pain, my hurt, and my bitterness.

I know some people experience instantaneous deliverance from their pain, hurt, and bitterness when they choose to forgive. That was not my experience. It wasn't instant. I prayed for a long time—a long, long time involving many, many prayers—asking God to take away the bitter, negative feelings and the anger I had toward my dad. I asked God to help me forgive my dad—to help me to even want to forgive him. Knowing how much God had done for me—all the sins He had forgiven—I knew God was able to help me. How could I withhold forgiveness from others when God had forgiven me so much? But I would be lying if I said it was easy.

The breaking point came the day God did a miracle. I decided to contact my dad, and my dad came for a visit. Seeing him that first time was beyond difficult, and I wondered if God really knew what He was doing by allowing this to happen. I was faced with the pain of neglect, the deep feelings of rejection, hopelessness, and anger that were all mixed up in my relationship with this man. God—and I know without a doubt it had to be Him—began to restore the relationship with my dad.

After one of the hardest conversations I have ever had, I knew God had given me the forgiveness in my heart for this man I once hated. We were able to talk, to laugh, to spend time together without the anger and the hurt. God had answered my many prayers. God changed my heart to be able to start to love my dad again.

He was, after all, a man who was himself broken and needed God in his life too. The process of restoration took a long time, but it started that day when God put the thought in my mind that there was a *possibility* that my dad and I could start to build a relationship again.

Another of the many important lessons God revealed to me after my conversion was that my love for money was not going to co-exist well in my relationship with Him.

The Bible declares,

"No one can serve two masters, either he will hate the one and love the other; you cannot serve both God and money,"

~Luke 16:13

One of the first things I had to lay down after my surrender to Christ was my money mindset. I was on a path to become a successful businessman, but God had other plans.

Instead of getting more money, God sent me to seminary!

Instead of money, I was going into ministry.

Through seminary, I learned that giving is more blessed than getting. I learned to put others' concerns ahead of my own, and I learned that God is my Provider, not my paycheck.

God provided in those days in ways that were amazing. My mom was even surprised at what God did in those days. Provision would come in creative ways—a family friend surprised me with a monetary gift before I left for seminary, a check in the mailbox, an unexpected package, and military discounts at various stores and other unexpected places. God did those things to remind me that He provided for me every step of the way.

Money was not an object to be worshipped, it was a tool God used to build my faith. A tool He asked me to give away when it didn't make sense, and a tool that had to be used with an open hand and not a closed fist. Remember the day I waded into the fountain and took other people's wish pennies? I am humbled to say that I do not take others' dreams now, but I do pick up change when I find it laying on the ground. The pennies that I find now remind me that God provides for me, and sometimes, He leaves pennies from heaven just to make sure that I remember where my trust lies—in Him and not in the money in my pocket.

Another important impact of seminary was learning about missions. I had been on missions trips with Campus Crusade, but I built friendships with men and women who were going to other countries to be missionaries long-term. Just like soldiers, they went to protect souls, but they do it with the Word of God and by sharing the Good News of Jesus Christ.

Remembering those people cheering for me from the curbside that homecoming day in Johnson City, I started to reach out and cheer on some of the missionaries I knew. I wanted them to know they were supported, encouraged, loved and prayed for—even if they were far away. When social media opened up avenues to communicate with them beyond letters, I signed up. I wanted those missionaries to know that God had brought them to my mind, laid them on my heart, and I was remembering them in prayer and encouraging them to keep on point.

Who is it that you can support and encourage, even if they live in another state, or are on another continent? Support them from the curb, just like those who were cheering us when we came home that day at Ft. Bragg. They need it, and we need to remember them too.

God also showed me during my time at seminary that underdogs come in all shapes and sizes and not just in sports. Before the desert, when it came to the homeless—I pretty much assumed that they didn't want to work, and I didn't have any empathy whatsoever.

Why would they choose to live like that?

How could they let themselves get to that low point in life?

After sixteen days in the desert with only one shower, I realized that sometimes life throws things at us that we were not prepared to deal with, and some people do not have the power to push through. My heart began to soften toward those who were less fortunate, those who were kicked while they were down and didn't have options or support systems like I do. This softening in my life was a preparation for what God would do next, and it was a good thing He taught me this while I was in seminary—I might have missed this had things gone according to my original plan.

This is a good reminder that even when things don't go according to plan—it can still be a blessing.

God even brought the BC—*birth control*—glasses to mind when I was at seminary. While I still need physical corrective lenses to this day, the Lord did show me that having spiritual vision is way more important.

I learned that God is always at work all around us. One of the greatest tragedies of life is the inability to see through God's perspective. My prayer is to be sensitive to the Holy Spirit and to see how God is at work and how He is calling me to join Him. I want a sensitivity to the Holy Spirit, to follow His leading and to kill off my selfish, sinful desires that blur my vision of what is right and wrong.

Being focused on loving God first and then loving others gives us the direction and clarity we need to be the good people He has called us to be (Ephesians 2:10). Perspective is key. God used this shift in my perspective to see people differently, and He blessed me during this time with the love of my life.

I met Trish, and we found that we were both passionate about helping others. God allowed us to date, marry, and begin a family, and I truly believe that I would have missed out on the biggest blessings of my life if I hadn't learned to see life differently.

Full Circle

I have often thought about my time in the desert. Occasionally I think about Reghed and the conversations we had. I recall pondering then about who could I help once I got home and where would I make a difference.

The answers to those questions came a few years after I returned home, but they were quite different than what I expected. While my dad had been absent in the beginning of my life, he would become fully present at the end of his.

My dad's life had spiraled out of control after we saw him at Ft. Bragg. He was decommissioned because of his assault on April, and then his life nosedived. His second wife left him, he wound up homeless—a member of a group I had despised earlier in my life—and then he developed Parkinson's.

Now God was giving me the opportunity to come alongside my dad and try to help him. Mom supported me, even though she kept her distance from my dad. She encouraged me to do what the Lord was telling me to do, and she never told me I was crazy.

April and I went to Washington, D.C. and helped him move his stuff out of a storage unit. He had nowhere to go, but God worked it out for him to come live with me and my wife and family. This was no small miracle, as the thought of having my dad anywhere near me just a few years prior would have filled me with disgust. But God had done such a work in my life that I was able to willingly offer my dad a place to live.

He lived on the second floor of our house, and we cooked for him, did his laundry, and became his primary caretakers. Thankfully, my wife was a trooper. She knew God was doing this in our lives, and she put up with me and loved my dad too.

One day I heard a big thud. That started the process of hearing a thud almost daily. At first we just assumed it was a onetime fall, but it turned into a daily occurrence. Dad could still walk, but he wasn't totally honest with us about what was happening, so it took a bit of investigating to find out what was going on. It was at that point we realized he needed more help than we could provide, and we began the arduous task of finding a good place for him to live with assistance.

After much effort, we finally got him placed in an assisted living home. He only lasted there a week before the Parkinson's became too much for the care they could provide. It was a difficult time for all of us, and Dad did not take it well.

My birthday fell in the middle of all this transition, and in an effort to keep our relationship positive, I suggested he could take me out for a steak dinner for my birthday.

He said, "No, I am saving my money for retirement."

After all these years, he still wasn't willing to spend a measly forty dollars or to spend that time with me.

I was hurt. After all the birthdays he had missed when I was growing up, I thought it would be a great opportunity for him to do something nice for me, to realize he had missed out on so much. I could feel all the bitterness welling up in my heart. I was shocked that after all this time, he still was more focused on himself than anyone else.

Thankfully, God intervened in my heart and once again showed me the value of forgiveness. God also reminded me that grace cannot be earned—it is freely given. I once again found myself asking God to help me forgive my dad and to extend grace to him.

Despite a long waiting list and mountain of red tape—I know now that God intervened—I was able to get my dad placed in the VA nursing home. Tyler and the staff made his time there the absolute best that it could possibly be. I am thankful for the five-star treatment that was provided at the VA nursing home.

It is possible my dad may hold the record for being the longest living patient there. I visited frequently, and I was able to tell him that I loved him before he passed away. I am so thankful God gave me the grace to forgive my dad.

Near the end of his life, April and I were able to connect with my dad's half-brother, who thought that my dad had died in Vietnam. They had lost contact with each other because my dad had been adopted in the US by a man named David Weill.

It turns out my dad had been in an orphanage in Belgium as a result of his mother being a prisoner in the Auschwitz concentration camp in Poland, and his father being in a different concentration camp. His birth name was Sylvan Borisewitz.

I was able to arrange a phone call with his half-brother Gilbert from Belgium, and Gilbert got to talk to my dad! Unfortunately, because of his Parkinson's, my dad was not able to talk back, but he could hear and understand what Gilbert was saying. I felt helping him connect with family at the end of his life was an important part of his healing—and mine.

I visited frequently with my dad, who was like a newborn due to his illness. Everything had to be done for him. Helping to feed him and talk to him made it seem that life had come full circle for us. Had God not worked such a miracle of forgiveness in my heart, these times would have been torturous. But over time, God gave me the grace to forgive my dad. As a result of God working in my life and understanding the Love God has for us, I was able to extend that love to my dad. I was able to tell him that I loved him and was grateful for the time I had with him. I was thankful that I was able to walk the final days of his journey with him.

N.M.P.

The military uses a lot of abbreviations for things, and N.M.P. has become my mantra as I have looked at my life through God's perspective. N.M.P. stands for **Not My P**lan.

It was not my plan to grow up without a dad, and then wind up lovingly, willingly, take care of him until he passed.

It was not my plan to sign up for the military to help pay for school and then wind up being deployed.

Taking my mom into a war zone? N.M.P.

College taking seven years instead of four, and then going onto seminary?—N.M.P.

Things not working out with Heather, but then finding Trish and knowing God was in all of it?—N.M.P.

Going to seminary to be in full time ministry and ended up becoming a franchise owner of Steak 'n Shake?—N.M.P.

God having me in a place where I can do a lot of ministry through and because of Steak 'n Shake?—N.M.P.

Telling this story in printed form?—N.M.P.

But God has added two more letters to the acronym through the years—BG. But God.

Proverbs 19:21 says:

"Many are the plans in a person's heart, but it is the Lord's purpose that prevails."

God knew, even before I was born, that this was the story He wanted me to tell for His glory.

He has a story for you too.

I hope as you have read through what God did for me—bringing a kid and a single mom through some amazing things—you will be encouraged about your own life.

Where you are struggling, God is there.

Where you don't have hope, **B**ut **G**od.

He is at work, and He has not forgotten you.

When you struggle to find peace, to belong, to offer forgiveness, to find purpose and to tell your story—He is there.

As you march through your own desert, may you find God changing your mindsets and guiding you every step of the way. You may not be deployed with your mother, but you are loved by a heavenly Father who has planned every step and wants more than anything for you to be one of His—His child, His soldier, His friend.

I hope you find Him in your desert—your personal war zone—but especially in your heart, today.

Epilogue

Where are we now?

Time has passed since Desert Storm, and my mom and I have had many plot twists in our journey. I finished school at East Tennessee State University and then headed to Mid-America Baptist Theological Seminary. I was planning to be in full time ministry and received a master's of Divinity.

During that time, Trish and I got married, and we have since been blessed with four children. We moved to Murfreesboro, Tennessee where we worked with CRU—the collegiate ministry that had been so impactful in my own life. We were there for six years, and we spent wonderful moments watching God impact college students' lives and prepare them for ministry as they prepared for their careers. We loved serving there, But God moved us on to our next adventure.

I moved into financial planning. I got licensed and worked hard. I hated it.

I would rather dig ditches in the desert than keep selling financial services.

I moved into telecommunications for a few years, then we bought a Cajun restaurant. Those were dark times. I dove into this business opportunity without praying about it, and we struggled for a year and a half with no income. The restaurant did not earn a single dollar. Thankfully, my wife had a job. I learned, again, that my trust must be in God and not myself or the dollar bill.

I was aware that my decisions affected my family too, and thankfully, God led me through these jobs to prepare me for the career and ministry that I have now. Full-time ministry was again at the forefront of my mind. I just had no idea that the *full-time* I was thinking of was not the *full-time* God had in mind. I thought work and ministry had to be two separate things.

I was pretty discouraged after that year and a half. In the exact moment I was desperate and needed help, God showed up in the most unexpected way. I was at a soccer banquet for my son, and a man I had just met told me about the Steak 'n Shake Franchise Partner program. If you are willing to work hard, put in sweat equity, and hit four specific goals, then you could become a franchise owner.

I prayed this time. I prayed a lot. Our main competition was a highly famous chicken place across the street, and I was going to have to sell my Tacoma truck to buy in. God opened all the doors, and I went to training in another city. I took the extra bunkbed mattress from my son's room and slept in my mother-in-law's Kia. I used the shower at the local gym while I was there.

Thankfully, God had used the time in the desert to teach me to appreciate the things He was doing in my life, and I was grateful that I didn't have to go sixteen days without a shower!

The Lord worked, I met the four specific goals, and I became the humble owner of a fabulous Steak 'n Shake location on March 25, 2020—the day after the dining room shut down due to Covid.

The Lord uses Steak 'n Shake every day to bless someone, to give me the opportunity to share His love, to give others a second chance through employment, and to have the money mindset to look for opportunities to bless others. Not My Plan, But God.

And my mom—she came home from the desert and continued to work as a nurse. She eventually retired and now operates Birdsong Sanctuary, a place where people can come visit, stay, and find some peace and solitude. She enjoys giving people a place to be out in nature and find time to relax. She has opened the sanctuary to musicians, couples, and veterans who want to come out and enjoy good music in a bed-&-breakfast-type atmosphere. This place looks like an old barn, but my mom completely redid the inside, and it is unique and beautiful. God took our journey in the desert and gave us life lessons that give hope, joy, and peace to me and my mom and to those who are reading our story now.

†††

I used to think life was divided into work and ministry. The Lord used my journey to show me that everything in life—work, family, church—is ministry. All of your life can be ministry too, if you surrender to God and what He wants to do in your life. God is at work all around us, and He allows us to be a part of it. We find hope and peace when we join in with Him.

If you are ever in middle Tennessee, stop by and see me at Steak 'n Shake. I will show you the picture of me and my mom in the desert. It is hanging on the wall in my restaurant to remind me that the lessons I learned were not my plan, but His plan, and He is good.

Acknowledgements

I want to thank my wife, Trish, who has supported this dream of writing my story. She wouldn't let me quit. She and our four children inspire me on a daily basis to be a better man, a better Christian, a better husband, and a better father. Their support means the world to me.

A very special thank you to my mom. To this day she doesn't make excuses, and she finds a way to make things happen. She sees life as a series of opportunities instead of obstacles, and I am forever grateful for her because she helped me learn to persevere by example. Thanks, Mom!

To every soldier who has served, is serving, and will serve our great country. Thank you!

To those who have lost hope in life, to those who need to be forgiven, and to those that need to offer forgiveness—my prayer is that this book will be a blessing to you.

I have had a desire to write this book for some time, but it wasn't until I met Tammy Chandler who encouraged, persevered, and helped me facilitate this book and make it a reality.

I want to thank the publishing team for walking me through the process of publishing and making this story a printed book. I could not have come this far without them all.

And I want to thank the Lord Jesus, who walked me through the desert and brought me to the best decision of my life—finding hope in Him. May He receive all the glory for writing my life story and loving me through every part.

His forgiveness is real. His hope is amazing. And His love is beyond comprehension! If you haven't experienced it for yourself, you don't know what you're missing.

David W. Weill III is a husband, father, public speaker, a franchise owner of Steak 'n Shake, and above all else, a follower of Christ. He came to know Christ through the ministry of Cru at the age of 23.

He graduated from ETSU with a bachelor's degree and later earned his Master of Divinity (MDiv) degree from Mid-America Baptist seminary. David and his wife Trish have been married since 2000. They have four children and reside in Middle Tennessee.

David earned the rank of Eagle Scout while in his teens and is proud to have served with the 912th MASH unit during Desert Storm. When he is not working or spending time with family, he enjoys golf and tennis and participating in obstacle course races— Tough Mudders and Spartans.

Also Available From

WordCrafts Press

Against Every Hope
Bonnie Tinsley

An Introspective Journey
Paula Sarver

Chronicles of a Believer
Don McCain

Confounding the Wise
Dan Kulp

Morning Mist
Barbie Loflin

www.wordcrafts.net